Agile means more than just being flexible. In instructional design, Agile is a disciplined flexibility, geared toward delivering the most essential product, responding to the most important changes, and constantly fine-tuning the needs and deliverables as a project develops. Based on an information technology industry model first documented in 2001 and popularized by books such as Eric Ries's *Lean Startup* and Michael Allen's *Leaving ADDIE for SAM*, Agile is used to respond to rapidly changing business requirements that shift even before the project is complete, and to address the plague of time and money spent on projects that fail to deliver a return on investment (ROI).

In this *TD at Work*, you will learn how to:

- Identify business goals.

- Use the traditional Agile approach to define the scope of a project.

- Leverage the LLAMA approach to define the scope of a project.

- Break your work down into easy to manage tasks.

- Use iterative development to refine a project's deliverables.

WHY AGILE?

Agile helps manage the time and budget invested in a project. It also helps project managers better target the deliverables required to meet the project's goals. This *TD at Work* will show you how to manage instructional systems design (ISD) and development projects using Agile project management, with an emphasis on the Lot Like Agile Methods Approach (LLAMA), which is designed specifically for instructional projects.

Why should we use a project management method derived from the information technology (IT) industry? To a certain extent the process of developing software and the process of developing training are parallel. They face many of the same types of project stakeholders: sponsors, subject matter experts (SMEs), developers, users, and learners. They also face many of the same types of problems: SMEs who

aren't dedicated, ever-changing business needs, and lack of clearly defined requirements. LLAMA makes some key adjustments to the mainstream Agile approach to account for the fact that training development is different from IT in some small—but important—aspects, notably:

- The syntax and structure of learning objectives differ from that of user requirements.

- Instructional designers are more likely to work on multiple projects than software engineers.

Agile and LLAMA work with any learning medium, whether you're designing classroom instruction, virtual training, e-learning, m-learning, or learning platforms. Agile works best for projects with clear (even if they're moving) start and end dates and deliverables. However, Agile does not work well with support functions, such as LMS help desk support, or the ongoing delivery of classroom curricula.

IDENTIFY A BUSINESS GOAL

Most project management methodologies and instructional design approaches suggest that you understand the business goal for the project before you get started. The Agile project management method, and the LLAMA method in particular, is no different in this respect. Much has been written on the need to tie a project into business goals (such as *Making the Financial Case for Performance Improvement* by Clare Novak and *Strategic Learning Alignment* by Rita Mehegan Smith), so in this *TD at Work* I'll share just a few tips to get you started.

When connecting your training with business goals that are, in turn, tied to business strategies, think big. Connecting the project's goals to a greater vision for the organization helps the project sponsors, SMEs, and the project team stay motivated when project crises arise. This project management technique also helps with instructional design because you'll be able to make this connection for the learners in your course.

WHAT DO WE REALLY MEAN BY AGILE?

At least four different uses of the word agile are active in the training world. While there is some overlap, knowing which agile you're using is important.

Content Agility is the capability to deliver learning material in a variety of formats. Think of this as a "write once, publish many" approach with the same content and structure being delivered through multiple platforms. Most content management systems and higher order content authoring systems allow for content agility.

Learning Agility is a person's ability to handle new problems and challenges based on prior learning and experience. It's essential for effective leadership and innovation, and can be fostered by an organization's culture around learning and growth.

AGILE Instructional Design is a design approach to a learning project with five stages: align, get set, iterate and implement, leverage, and evaluate. AGILE is designed to support learning teams as they rapidly deploy both formal learning and complementary performance-support mechanisms for informal learning.

Agile Project Management is a method for managing a creative project process, one in which team members experiment and observe to improve a product as it is developed. Agile project management works well when the design and development involves creative and complex decisions, when the specifications may not be well defined, and when business needs shift. To handle all this change, the Agile project management approach builds deliverables in small increments, releases usable products frequently, and uses those releases to gather feedback. LLAMA—the Lot Like Agile Management Approach—is a modification of the traditional Agile techniques to support instructional design and development projects.

This *TD at Work* focuses on Agile project management and LLAMA, although any of the other types of agile can be incorporated into the designs of a project managed this way.

Most business strategies fall into one of four broad categories:

- increasing revenue or income
- decreasing costs (including the costs of legal or ethical non-compliance)
- improving product or service quality (including the ability of customers to engage with the product or service)
- expanding the capacity of the organization and its people.

You should define the business goal in as much detail as is useful for the project effort. Be sure that vague terms such as "improve" and "reduce" have shared meaning across all the stakeholders. Some organizations use SMART (specific, measurable, attainable, realistic, and timely) goals or other criteria to define outcomes. In other environments, stakeholders will bristle at the thought of putting too fine a point on things. Following the organization's lead on this will further help to align the project with the organization's cultural context.

START WITH THE LEARNER IN MIND

When kicking off a project using an Agile methodology such as LLAMA, start by defining a primary learner persona (PLP). Instructional design projects typically start with an audience analysis, which provides a detailed look at the range of learners, their skills, and their needs for your project.

Defining the PLP

The PLP is something quite different from the audience analysis. When you define a PLP, you focus your view on a single, usually fictitious, learner for the project. The primary learner is often an iconic member of the broader audience, and is recognizable to stakeholders as a realistic portrayal of a typical individual. Although it is possible to identify the PLP with an actual person, you should avoid doing so. The PLP is defined in much greater detail than most audience analyses in terms of personal characteristics, motivations, family, recreational activities, professional goals, and level of comfort with technology (particularly with e-learning projects). It is given a name and often a photo. A sample PLP description can be found in the Example of a Primary Learner Persona sidebar.

> THE PRIMARY LEARNER IS OFTEN AN ICONIC MEMBER OF THE BROADER AUDIENCE, AND IS RECOGNIZABLE TO STAKEHOLDERS AS A REALISTIC PORTRAYAL OF A TYPICAL INDIVIDUAL.

Why create a persona with this much detail? By identifying the PLP as a realistic person, the project team and project sponsors have an easier time relating the PLP to an actual learner. In the throes of day-to-day project activities, it is easy to get lost in the details of screen layout, instructional notes, job aids, LMS compatibility, and the hundreds of other things instructional designers need to worry about. It is helpful to think of the PLP as a member of the project team, guiding instructional designers through a variety of decisions and offering both SMEs and stakeholders a clear rationale for those decisions.

You may create multiple personas during a project, but you should define and select one to be the primary persona. This helps keep the project from being all things to all people, which often really means all sorts of things for no one in particular. Defining a single PLP does not mean you are excluding other types of learners from using the same course and content. Instead, when the tough decisions need to be made about your project, your team can use the PLP's traits as a guide on how to proceed.

Defining the PLP is one of the earliest activities in a project kickoff session. Both SMEs and stakeholders should be included in the process. Instructional designers may guide the session with questions, but the business client should drive the responses. For this exercise, you'll want to have four to six flipcharts, whiteboard sections, or worksheet columns—one for each

EXAMPLE OF A PRIMARY LEARNER PERSONA

Name: Geoffrey
Age: 42

Geoff has spent the last five years of his career as a project manager in the IT department and has great aspirations to someday become the director of IT. Prior to working at his current company, he held IT positions at several small to mid-size companies throughout the Northeast. While he feels comfortable in his current role and enjoys being a leader to his six direct reports, he knows that to move forward in his career he will need to stay current on cutting-edge tools and continue learning new skills so that he looks smart and competent, not just overbearing.

Putting in 45 to 50 hours a week plus driving 45 minutes to get to the office each day means that Geoff's wife, Karen, does most of the chauffeuring of their two kids, Alex (10) and Bethany (8), to their various extracurricular activities. On the weekends when he's not at work, Geoff spends most of his time doing work around the house. If he's lucky he'll have time to check in on his Fantasy Football team, but usually he gives up after a few weeks and lets the roster sit through the end of the season, leaving it up to luck if he wins the pool of money that he and his college buddies contributed to.

Geoff likes it when he has the opportunity to complete his required training and development activities via e-learning because it means that he can go at his own pace and fit it into his busy schedule wherever and whenever time allows. Even better is when Geoff can watch and learn using his shiny new tablet, which he almost always has with him.

> IT IS HELPFUL TO THINK OF THE PLP AS A MEMBER OF THE PROJECT TEAM, GUIDING INSTRUCTIONAL DESIGNERS THROUGH A VARIETY OF DECISIONS AND OFFERING BOTH SMES AND STAKEHOLDERS A CLEAR RATIONALE FOR THOSE DECISIONS.

PROJECT KICKOFF AGENDA

- Introduce participants, roles, and agenda.

- Participate in an icebreaker or perspective gathering on the topic.

- Define the business problem(s) and goal(s).

- Define the learner personas and select the primary learner persona.

- Begin action mapping.

- Describe success in terms of action items and emotive aspects for the learners.

- Scope out phases of work and iteration approaches.

- Define the assessment criteria.

- Determine reviewer and SME needs throughout the project.

- Identify post-training performance support needs.

- Define technical specifications and requirements.

- Conduct risk analysis.

- Determine project budget and timeline boundaries.

- Close with next steps and follow-up action items.

learner persona that you'll develop. At a high level, start defining the learners. Ask questions to generate more details about each persona, and work toward a consensus-based definition before moving on to the next learner. Most projects will have three to six types of learners. You'll often find new and interesting questions as you go, so make sure to answer them for any previously defined learners so you have comparable descriptions.

Choosing the PLP

Next you'll help the project sponsors decide which of the personas will be the primary one for the project. In some cases, it will be remarkably clear which persona to choose. In other cases, deciding the PLP will be the predominant discussion during the kickoff process. The arguments made about which persona should be the PLP are often more useful to instructional designers than the actual choice made in the end. This process will call upon all of your best facilitation skills.

How the primary persona is chosen varies from project to project. Here are a few examples from actual projects:

- In a concussion education course for coaches, the client chose the high school football coach persona over the girls' soccer coach or the recreational flag football coach personas. The client's public health educators felt that a school's sports culture and attitudes about concussions were led by the football program. Messages aimed at the football coach would be accepted by other coaches, but not necessarily vice versa.

- In a course about environmental records management for a global chemicals manufacturer, the client chose an employee who represented those who worked in the office, a minority population for the PLP. Although 70 percent of the workers were located in plants, these employees had a long history of excellent compliance and years of experience with the company's procedures. The 30 percent of employees who worked in the office had a shorter tenure with the company and less daily interaction with records, making them a critical population to reach.

- In a supervisory skills class for a food manufacturing company, the client felt that 50 percent of the learner population would be eager to learn more and improve their skills, while the other 50 percent would be dismissive of learning new soft skills. Since the class would be taught in five quarterly sessions, the client wanted to be sure that supervisors would continue to come to all of the sessions. The skeptical learner was chosen as the PLP because getting him to both apply the skills and come back for more training was the biggest challenge the project faced.

CASE STUDY:
THE PLP—WHY WE CHOSE WHO WE CHOSE

During a recent project kickoff session for a client, my team and I started the process of narrowing in on a learner persona for a compliance course on records management that focused on the policies around keeping or destroying certain business documents.

There were two main populations in this company: office workers (HR, sales, legal, and finance) and plant workers (who actually make the company product). Within the office there were some research and development workers who shared similar traits with the workers in the plants. Conversely, some plant people kept track of important documents related to environmental health and safety—functions often performed by people in an office setting. Everyone used a computer during some or all of the workday.

So how did we determine the learner persona? When we asked the client how many workers were in each group, we discovered that plant personnel outnumbered office personnel by more than 2:1. This left us with more questions. Should the primary learner persona reflect the majority (plant) workers? Should the learner persona fit the profile of an office worker, such as a finance staff member handling very important records? Who were our primary learners? This was going to be difficult.

Just as we were about to concede that maybe this project had two primary learners, someone made an interesting observation. The client was a new company made up of components of an older, more established company. The people in the plants came from the legacy company, an organization with a very mature records process. In fact, these workers had been wondering when the new company was going to get an organized process for records management. The personnel in the office were new and some didn't even have a background in their company's industry.

I asked if perhaps we needed two courses after all: one for plant people, and one for office people. However, the client only had a budget for one course.

Then we asked the critical question: If this training failed, who was most at risk? The client knew at once that the office personnel were most at risk. They were the ones who didn't actually have the knowledge, habits, or culture around appropriate records management. And they had more different types of records than the plant employees, so their process was both newer to them and more complex. Even if the project failed, the personnel in the plant would be able to comply with the records management process without the training. The office personnel would not be able to do so.

We could then create a single learner persona. His name was Hans. He was a finance employee from Germany, in his late 20s, and had been with the company since it was formed three years ago. This was his first real job after college, and he may not stay with the company for long. He was eager to take online training.

Thinking we were done, we moved on to the action mapping part of the process. That's where it got interesting. We laid out all the actions that Hans would be taking on his way to meeting the business goals of: (a) being able to find the up-to-date files he needed quickly in order to meet customer and business needs, and (b) keeping the company out of legal trouble. When we looked back at those actions, we realized that there were many things that Hans needed to know that his colleagues in the plants didn't.

So, despite the fact that we could have built two courses with a PLP for plant workers and a PLP for office workers, we decided to build one comprehensive course with everything in it, and then slice out the parts that the plant personnel didn't need. That decision drove us to a very modular instructional design approach.

It's critical to note that the persona is not specifically mentioned within the course. The goal is to reach learners most like the PLP, but not necessarily to exclude the other learners. Take the food manufacturing company example—the facilitators in the session didn't announce that they felt the learners would be skeptical or say anything that would tip the learners off to the true PLP. Instead, the course design ensured that the skeptical learners would have a positive experience and learn easy-to-apply skills that could be used right away. Activities were designed so that no one was made to feel silly, no one had to share difficult or embarrassing stories, and everything felt practical. This way, the course ensured that every learner had a positive experience, even those who may have been more difficult to reach.

DEFINE SCOPE WITH LEARNER STORIES

The next step for instructional designers is to define the requirements, the scope of the project, and the course objectives. By using Agile, you can tackle these steps by creating user stories. The subject of a user story could be the PLP or some other stakeholder related to the trainings, such as managers, division heads, the LMS administrators, or even customers.

The Traditional Agile Approach

A user story is an independent unit of scope that can be prioritized, assigned, developed, and tested along the project's path to completion. During a project kickoff session, you'll brainstorm user stories with all the stakeholders, project sponsors, SMEs, and instructional team members contributing. You should conduct this session live and face-to-face if feasible. Record the ideas the kickoff group generates in a visual way. If you're working together, use 3x5 cards, sticky notes, or a whiteboard to record your ideas. If you're working virtually, use a digital tool that all members can see and use. Challenge participants to define a meaningful "why" for each idea or card. A card without a "why" could represent a very low priority idea or is not necessary at all.

It is important to generate more ideas than you think you'll need. Often the best ideas come out after the team has an opportunity to reflect, add to, and combine other ideas. Remember to accept ideas from everyone. Later on you'll have the opportunity to choose the ones that are most meaningful to the project.

As you work through this process, you may see patterns and logical groupings emerge. If you use cards or sticky notes you can move them around easily to fit these patterns. Sometimes you'll see a timeline emerge. Other times the patterns will evolve around different groups of people who get involved at different levels. Sometimes you'll see the opportunity for a phased project implementation that meets critical needs first, and other needs later on. Following the story metaphor, the Agile term for a large group of related stories is an epic.

If you were building a new Internet search engine, you and the project's sponsors and experts might brainstorm a set of user stories along these lines:

- As a user, I want a large number of web search results all on the same page so I can scroll through quickly and see them all.

- As an advertiser, I want to place ads on pages where people who search for things related to my product are browsing.

- As the infrastructure manager, I want to display only 15 results on each page so the engine has time to process the rest of the results in the background.

- As the product manager, I want to know what kinds of searches are popular so I can continue to improve the search engine's service.

The list above highlights some key points about user stories. The first is the format: a user story has a structure that identifies the who, the what, and, perhaps of critical importance, the why for each requirement.

As a _____WHO_____,
I want _____WHAT_____
so I can _____WHY_____.

The next key point to note about user stories is that multiple types of people have needs that must be met by this project. In the example, we have the user, of course, but we also have advertisers, the infrastructure manager, and the product manager, all of whom have needs. This is an opportunity for the project sponsors and team to prioritize stories for maximum impact across all the key stakeholders.

> **A USER STORY IS AN INDEPENDENT UNIT OF SCOPE THAT CAN BE PRIORITIZED, ASSIGNED, DEVELOPED, AND TESTED ALONG THE PROJECT'S PATH TO COMPLETION.**

Some of the user stories in our example compete with each other. Users want a long list of results to scroll through, but the infrastructure manager only wants to display 15 results on the page at a time. This is another opportunity to weigh the needs and identify priorities.

The INVEST-U criteria will help you write stories that are maximally useful for project planning. Each story should be:

- Independent. It can be implemented without influencing other stories. For example, the ad placement story and popular search results story are independent of each other.

- Negotiable. The story can be traded or negotiated with other stories when determining project scope or phases.

- Valuable. The story has meaning or purpose for one or more stakeholders. If a story has no value, discard it so you can focus on ones that do have value.

- Estimable. The story is defined such that designers and developers can estimate how long it will take to produce. This is particularly helpful when assigning timelines and budgets to projects.

- Small. Developers more easily estimate the production time of a story with a small and well-defined scope. Large and poorly defined stories should be broken down into smaller chunks before proceeding.

- Testable. In the information technology and Agile project management world, "testable" refers to our ability to test or verify that the task has been completed, while in the instructional design world "testable" refers to the ability to test or verify the learning.

- Understandable. The story has been documented in a way that can be shared with and easily understood by others. While this seems like a shockingly obvious requirement at first, it is still an important factor to consider. Stories that are not understandable are those that may not have shared value or meaning across the organization. As a result, these stories are often lower in priority for the project team to deliver on than other stories.

The LLAMA Approach

Creating user stories with the traditional Agile approach and INVEST-U criteria works particularly well for projects involving performance support tools, mobile application design, virtual learning environment scoping, or other tools being developed to do something for the learners.

In the instructional design process, traditional Agile story mapping breaks down, or is at least rather cumbersome, when it is applied to training a learner to do something. Using traditional Agile story mapping for training projects tends to result in very information-driven courses to the great frustration of the instructional design team and, ultimately, the learner. This is because the structure of the traditional Agile user story is somewhat different from the structure of a performance-based learning objective. This leads us to an essential deviation from the traditional Agile process that we use within the LLAMA approach. Cathy Moore's action mapping process uses proposed user actions to generate stories for project planning.

Action mapping begins with the business goal definition, often in response to a business problem to be solved. During the kickoff session with project stakeholders, SMEs, and the instructional design team, the actions that the primary learner (PLP) will take when successfully attaining the business goal are identified. Define these actions using verbs and enough description to meet the "U" in the INVEST-U criteria. When actions are visible, measurable, and understandable, you create the framework for a very action-focused and interesting course.

Before jumping into the instructional design work of the project definition, take time to review the actions you've identified and start doing some basic scoping for the project. Are there actions that can be grouped together as like skills? Which actions are expected of beginners and which are more suitable for experts? Are there actions that are supported in other courses already? Which ones are tied to decisions that will be made in the near future, for which we should hold off building training right now (if we can)? Is it possible that training is not the answer? One foundation to a successful project is to know what not to do, and action mapping at this stage of the process is an excellent place to start laying that out.

The action map continues with the remaining actions—those that haven't been deemed out of scope, not solvable through training, or simply not feasible at this time. Here's where the instructional design comes in. For each action you will identify ways in which learners can practice or interact with the content in some meaningful fashion. Generate a few ideas for each so that you can choose the best modality for the situation, scoping the project's size, timeline, and budget. The practice activities in the course may support multiple actions, just as a single action may have multiple practice opportunities in the course. A one-to-one relationship does not need to be maintained.

In some cases, this part of the exercise is done with the stakeholders and SMEs in the room. The action map, together with the primary learner persona, helps everyone understand the scope of the project and the level of skill learners need to attain in order to meet the business goal. Thus, the practice activities become a logical next step for the group.

In many other cases, I've found that this step in instructional design work is best completed by the project team and presented to the project sponsor at a subsequent meeting. This allows the

> FOR EACH ACTION YOU WILL IDENTIFY WAYS IN WHICH LEARNERS CAN PRACTICE OR INTERACT WITH THE CONTENT IN SOME MEANINGFUL FASHION.

instructional design team more time to gather ideas before presenting an approach for the course, and it focuses the time and efforts of the noninstructional designer members on the information they are most uniquely qualified to provide during the kickoff session.

The final component of the action map is determining what information is needed to complete the practice activities. Instead of merely converting old slide decks and instructor guides into a new course, the only information requested from SMEs and sponsors is the information that is directly related to the project at hand. This keeps the information in the course focused on the actions the learner needs to use on the job. This will guide you to more focused, and perhaps more interesting, training delivery. As with the practice activities, the knowledge required for the course does not have to be in a one-to-one relationship with the practice opportunities.

The job of the instructional design team is to define, develop, and present the practice activities and supporting knowledge in a meaningful way in the course. Each practice activity represents a learner story in the LLAMA version of Agile project management, meets the INVEST-U criteria, and can be used for the purposes of estimating, scoping, and planning the project.

CHUNKING THE WORK EFFORT

In a process analogous to chunking knowledge to make it easier to learn, the next step—whether in the traditional Agile or in LLAMA—is to break the project down into smaller chunks to make it more workable. There are two parts to this step.

The first part is to define and scope out the broad pieces of a larger project with an eye toward delivering pieces of the work quickly and frequently. There are a number of ways to do this: by importance, by audience, by language, by timeframe of when it's needed, and so on. It's important to break the project down into manageable pieces, with each piece having its own timeline. To create a timeline you will need to know the total amount of time that the organization considers reasonable for the project, the relative priority of each piece of the project, and how much work effort will be needed to complete those pieces.

Splitting a project into small workable pieces involves taking each of the user stories within the project scope and breaking them down into the tasks required to complete them. For example, some of the tasks required to create a clickable hotspot safety violation activity in an e-learning course include:

- Gather the list of safety violations to be shown in this activity.

- Identify a location for a photo shoot.

- Schedule the SME, the location, and the photographer for the photo shoot.

- Complete the photo shoot.

- Select and edit the photos.

- Create low-fidelity hotspot activity mockup.

- Send the mockup to the SME and request review.

Notice that the list only includes the tasks that are to be performed by the learning project team, not the tasks to be completed by others (most notably, the SME's review). Also, unlike the user stories, the tasks above do not strictly adhere to the INVEST-U criteria. For example, they are not independent—you cannot edit the photos before they are taken. Nor are they negotiable—you cannot trade the task of identifying a location for a photo shoot with selecting and editing a photo. However, each of the tasks is valuable, estimable, small, testable, and understandable.

Estimate Each Work Task

Next you'll need to estimate the time it will take to complete each of the work tasks you've identified. This will be your confirmation (or lack thereof) of the broad estimates you and your

team made at the project kickoff and, as such, it can provide an important validation point and opportunity to check in with the project sponsor before proceeding.

Agile imposes some significant rigor on the estimating process, because it is at this point in the project when the individual team members begin to interact with the work to be done. On larger projects the entire team participates in an initial work estimate. On smaller projects the person responsible for completing the work is the one responsible for estimating it. If the person responsible for completing the work doesn't have the experience to make an appropriate estimate, a more experienced or knowledgeable person can provide assistance.

The number of hours of work required to complete each task is estimated with no padding or contingency. While it may seem wise to round up or add a little bit of time to your estimate, during the course of an entire project this padding adds up considerably and leaves the team and project sponsors without a factual basis upon which to make decisions. Instead, recognize that this is just an estimate. This is perhaps the single most difficult thing to adapt to when implementing an Agile or LLAMA approach.

Agile has a built-in mechanism for handling uncertainty that makes padding the estimate unnecessary. Each hour of work is estimated in powers of two: 1, 2, 4, 8, 16, 32, and so forth. Some Agile methods use the Fibonacci sequence of numbers (numbers in the integer sequence 1, 2, 3, 5, 8, 13, 21, 34, and so forth) for estimating the length of time of a user story. Others simply use small, medium, large, and extra large as terms to describe their estimates, provided that they've defined these terms internally.

While it's inevitable that some tasks will take longer than estimated, that doesn't mean it's not worth exploring (or at least bearing in mind) why an estimate might have been wrong. Some common causes of inaccurate estimates include:

- doing more work than is required

- not having the right skills to do the work

- the task is not well-defined

- the task is misunderstood

- something about the work changed in the process of doing it

- something went wrong

- because it was just an estimate.

As a project manager, you'll want to create an environment on the Agile team in which it is safe to make mistakes in estimating. Many teams have a rule to communicate as soon as one knows an estimate is materially wrong. This information is of far more value earlier (when something can be done about it) than later. Correspondingly, the rule for the project manager is to immediately thank the bearer of the news about the estimate. Now the project manager knows more than he knew a few minutes before. Together, the team works out a response to this new information and, if needed, they communicate with the project sponsor.

When the tasks are small, it's easier to estimate them and you're likely to be more accurate. It's also easier to know when things are going wrong. This is simply because we have a better handle on smaller pieces of work, and fewer things can go awry along the way. Some project teams allow no tasks greater than eight hours. If a task estimate exceeds the eight-hour self-imposed limit, they break it down into smaller pieces.

Sometimes a task could be very nebulously defined such that it is impossible to estimate. If the task is to research the top 10 practices for mentoring new hire employees, an Internet search could yield a result in 0.36 seconds. On the other hand, a doctoral dissertation on the same topic could take three years. Who determines how long a task should take? In this case, how much the project sponsor values a particular task can influence the work estimate.

> **AS A PROJECT MANAGER, YOU'LL WANT TO CREATE AN ENVIRONMENT ON THE AGILE TEAM IN WHICH IT IS SAFE TO MAKE MISTAKES IN ESTIMATING.**

In my experience implementing LLAMA, my team found that the practice of estimating tasks and then paying attention to how long each one took was also a meaningful way to keep track of their own time and enforce responsible limits. By setting a time limit, you are less likely to tweak your work and take more time than it's really worth.

It's important to note that the estimates for each task are the estimates of the work effort it will take to complete it, not the duration of time over which it will be accomplished. The duration of the project is addressed in the planning of the work, and the estimate of the work effort is an essential component of that process.

PLAN THE WORK AND WORK THE PLAN

With a defined scope, project sponsor timeline, and budget, as well as the estimated work effort for each task, you are now ready to plan the work—and work the plan.

An Agile-based project is planned from both the top down and the bottom up, with adjustments as needed so that the schedule works for all parties.

You should develop a high-level plan for the top-down aspect of your work. The high-level plan takes into consideration the work estimate, the due date for the project, and the schedules of key people involved in the effort. Start planning by first noting any upcoming vacations, personnel changes, and project reassignments that could affect your team, then schedule the most work-heavy aspects of your project. For example, if a large part of your project requires you to create your own images or videos, consider all the factors that could affect the shoot. If you choose to shoot inside, consider the appropriate venue. If you choose to work outside, consider the weather and the time of year when you schedule your shoot.

Next, ask how long the reviewers will need to complete their part of the project so you can schedule that in as well. Some reviewers will block out a half day if they know in advance when they will be called upon. Others, particularly when

SMEs and reviewers are volunteers or there are a large number of them, will take weeks or months to complete their reviews. Typically a reviewer takes a week or two to provide feedback. Knowing the timeframe for a review often matters more than the actual amount of time it takes the reviewer to look over the work.

You'll then lay out a plan for frequent small reviews of the work, with sufficient time set aside for reviewers and SMEs to do their part. This is the broad arc of the project, and it is often organized by key activities happening each week. This high-level project schedule can be laid out next to the schedules for your team's other projects. This will help you as the project manager, and your peers, assign team members to projects and avoid having too many similar tasks lined up all at once. Creating a visual schedule for team members and stakeholders will help keep your work present in everyone's minds—and make it easy to make quick adjustments when needed. Whenever possible, keep this high-level schedule in physical format: cork boards, sticky notes, whiteboards, or even LEGO blocks. (See page 12 for an example of a corkboard format schedule.) A wide variety of Agile project management tools can be used to support virtual teams, although these tools have the disadvantage of a limited screen size across which to display many projects at once.

The following are examples of best practices for high-level scheduling:

- Avoid scheduling release dates for multiple projects all at once.

- Avoid scheduling many reviews for the same reviewers all at once.

- Allow for downtime or over-runs between projects.

- Encourage team members and fellow project managers to participate in high-level scheduling for the best allocation of resources and time.

- Remember that the project schedule is an estimate. The further out it goes, the less likely it is to be completely accurate, so plan accordingly.

- Share the high-level schedule frequently with project stakeholders, SMEs, and reviewers.

- Use code names to identify projects if having their schedules out in the open and visible might be a problem.

CREATING A VISUAL SCHEDULE FOR TEAM MEMBERS AND STAKEHOLDERS WILL HELP KEEP YOUR WORK PRESENT IN EVERYONE'S MINDS—AND MAKE IT EASY TO MAKE QUICK ADJUSTMENTS WHEN NEEDED.

Bottom-up project planning aligns tasks, team members, and resources with the broad top-down project schedule. If the goal for the current week is to deliver a high-level storyboard to the reviewers, then each of the week's tasks must support that goal. What's more, the team members must have at least as much time available to work on a project task as the estimated time to complete it. If the task estimates are greater than the time available, you need to change the scope of the work to fit the team's schedule, change the task's deadline, or add more team member resources.

Each team member should lay out her tasks on the week's schedule based on the time estimates. Be sure to account for standing meetings, days off work, and other job responsibilities as tasks are allocated. If there are tasks that don't fit within the week's schedule, put them in a pull-ahead pile so that if work is completed faster than estimated, everyone knows what should be worked on next. Write out the weekly tasks on a board for each project, with columns for the team members and rows for the days of the week. If using online tools, assign team members and dates to each task.

CORKBOARD FORMAT SCHEDULE

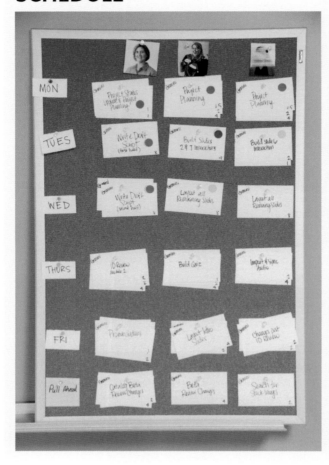

As the work is completed, its status is updated so that a visual and real-time status can be obtained at any time. Agile tasks are typically color coded to denote status. With the LLAMA approach, we use the following colors:

- No color: This task has not started.
- Yellow: This task is in progress.
- Green: This task is completed.
- Blue: Something is needed before this can be completed.
- Red: Something has gone wrong with this task.

These detailed weekly project plans are updated each week based on the work completed in the prior week and input from the project sponsor regarding priorities and changes. During the weekly update, changes are made to the high-level project plan are made to ensure that the two plans remain in sync.

With an Agile project management approach, it becomes very easy for team members to track their hours spent on a project at a task-by-task level because they are already doing this with work estimates. This supports allocations within organizations or direct billing by vendors on an hourly basis.

Daily stand-up meetings are also held with all members of the project team—including SMEs and project sponsors when appropriate. During the meeting, team members quickly report on the tasks they completed the day before, the planned tasks for the day, and any help they need from others. Each person's report should be very brief, allowing the entire team to get an update on statuses and activities without being too time-consuming.

ITERATIVE DEVELOPMENT

A hallmark of Agile project management is the iterative development approach, also known as successive approximation. In this approach, you release small, meaningful portions of your project to gather feedback and make changes to implement in the next round of work.

Many of us are in the business of building training to give both our learners and the organizations they work for a strategic competitive advantage. So it is important to get it right. Sometimes instructional designers bristle at the thought of 11th-hour changes to their projects. However, by expecting these changes, and accepting them willingly, your team can ensure that the training they deliver is up-to-the-minute. This isn't always easy, but it is essential.

Perhaps the best way to describe iterative development is to compare it to something more familiar—the ADDIE model that is typically drawn as a linear progression through five phases: analyze, design, develop, implement, and evaluate. (See the ADDIE Linear Model on page 13.) While

ADDIE LINEAR MODEL

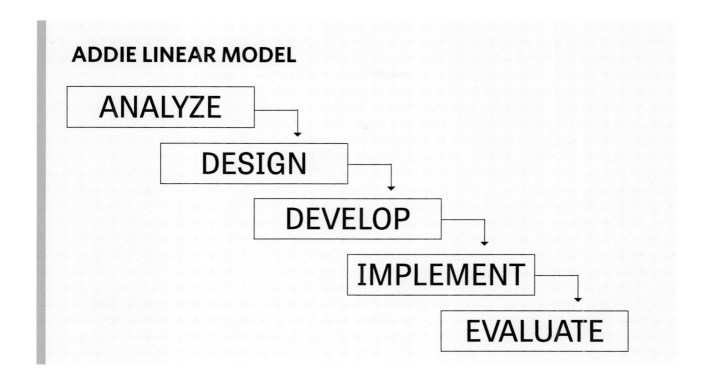

in an ideal world the ADDIE model's evaluate step leads directly into the next iteration of the linear progression, the realities of life in an organization with multiple pressing priorities means that this doesn't happen as often as it should.

In the LLAMA approach, the ADDIE steps are done in more rapid succession, completing several iterations in the same timeframe (as seen in the LLAMA Iterative Model on page 14). In that sense, the team doesn't wait until the very end of the project to get feedback from the sponsor, SMEs, and potential learners. The goal is to produce several iterations of the training, each of which is a usable version. The instructional design team benefits from feedback before the course is fully built so that changes can easily be made.

During each iteration, you'll release what's known as the minimum viable product, or MVP. The MVP is the simplest version of the deliverable that is still viable to release into the world–often to a very small subset of pilot testers or reviewers to get their feedback. During the scoping and planning phases of the project, you'll identify ways in which you can plan for releasable iterations and MVPs throughout the project. Iterations are typically released every two weeks to two months, depending on the scope of the project.

After each iteration is released, you receive feedback and make changes to the work. These changes are defined in terms of learner stories, or, in many cases, simply a list of things to revise. The team estimates the work effort associated with each change, confirms with the project sponsor that the adjustments are worth the work effort required to make them, and begins the planning and scheduling process for the new iteration.

There are several advantages to an iterative approach beyond the sheer value of gathering input to improve the work. It's an essential part of identifying and fixing errors early; whether they are errors in assumption, errors of omission, errors in style, or errors in fact. When you release a project in several small iterations, you always have something usable available for learners who cannot wait for the completed project for one reason or another. And, should the project get unceremoniously cancelled, you have a product of value to show for your efforts.

Early and frequent iterative releases also keep you and the project team from getting too far off track, both in terms of facts and scope, and in terms of project estimates because you're working with smaller durations of time. Should the organizational imperative underlying the training change during the project, you already

LLAMA ITERATIVE MODEL

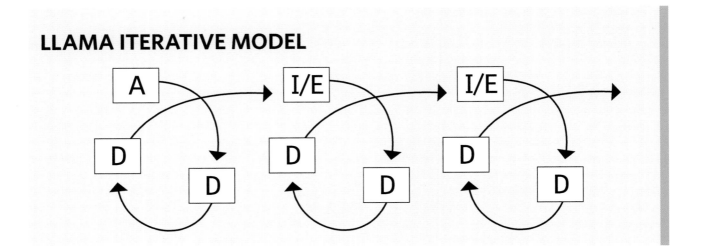

have a built-in communication mechanism with the project sponsor to learn about the change as soon as possible.

A common mistake is to require sign-off or commitment from reviewers and the project sponsor at each iteration. Unfortunately this sets the team up for struggle and possible failure. Requirements are constantly changing and we have a mandate to keep up with them, rather than resist them. Sign-off is a process for shutting down changes and closing doors behind you, rather than keeping them open and keeping up with the speed of change.

management—including learner personas, action mapping, work estimation and planning, iterations—and noting ways in which you can improve these processes, contributes to a higher likelihood of meeting learner needs, which, in the long run, is what it's all about.

CONCLUSION

Adopting an Agile methodology, whether it's LLAMA or another approach, won't guarantee faster or cheaper projects, or even better projects. It's no silver bullet. However, Agile will help instructional designers and developers meet the demands of constantly shifting organizational needs while moving toward a project's completion.

Most projects are really never done; we just stop working on them. With an Agile project, the sponsor decides what constitutes as done for the project. Until then, the team continues to produce iterations and phases of the work until the project timeline runs out, the budget runs dry, or there are no more meaningful things worth changing.

When you do finish a project, it is helpful to keep a list of things to change or improve the next time you use Agile to complete a project. Implementing all aspects of Agile project

Books

Allen, M. 2012. *Leaving ADDIE for SAM.* Alexandria, VA: ASTD Press.

Beck, K. 1999. *Extreme Programming Explained: Embrace Change.* Indianapolis: Addison-Wesley.

Robson, S. 2013. *Agile SAP: Introducing Flexibility, Transparency, and Speed to SAP Implementations.* Ely, UK: IT Governance Publishing.

Russell, L. 2000. *Project Management for Trainers: Stop Winging It and Get Control of Your Training Projects.* Alexandria, VA: ASTD Press.

Torrance, M. 2014. *A User's Guide to LLAMA, Agile Project Management for Learning, Iteration 2.0.* Chelsea, MI: TorranceLearning.

Articles

Sheridan, R. 2010. "Agile Explained: Secrets of Software Success." v7.0.

Torrance, M. 2014a. "All-Around Agility." *Training,* February.

——— 2014b. "Reconciling ADDIE and Agile." *Learning Solutions Magazine,* July 28.

———.2014c. "What Does It Mean to Be Agile?" *Learning Solutions Magazine,* April 21.

Websites

Beedle, M. et al. "Principles Behind the Agile Manifesto." Agile Manifesto. http://agilemanifesto.org/principles.html.

Fields, J. 2008. "User Story Estimation Techniques." InfoQ, June 30. www.infoq.com/articles/agile-estimation-techniques.

Moore, C. "Action Mapping: A Visual Approach to Training Design." Cathy Moore Blog. http://blog.cathy-moore.com/action-mapping-a-visual-approach-to-training-design.

STATEMENT OF OWNERSHIP, MANAGEMENT, AND CIRCULATION

1. PUBLICATION TITLE: TD at Work (formerly Infoline)
2. PUBLICATION NO. 2373-5570 (formerly 8755-9269)
3. FILING DATE: September 16, 2014
4. ISSUE FREQUENCY: Monthly
5. NO. OF ISSUES PUBLISHED ANNUALLY: 12
6. ANNUAL SUBSCRIPTION PRICE: $139.00 List $99.00 Members
7. COMPLETE MAILING ADDRESS OF KNOWN OFFICE OF PUBLICATION: ATD, 1640 King Street, Alexandria, VA 22314
8. COMPLETE MAILING ADDRESS OF HEADQUARTERS OR GENERAL BUSINESS OFFICE OF PUBLISHER: ATD, 1640 King Street, Alexandria, VA 22314
9. FULL NAMES AND COMPLETE MAILING ADDRESSES OF PUBLISHER, EDITOR, AND MANAGING EDITOR PUBLISHER: ASTD DBA Association for Talent Development (ATD) 1640 King Street, Alexandria, VA 22314
   EDITOR: Patty Gaul, MANAGING EDITOR: Ashley Slade
10. OWNERS FULL NAME: ASTD DBA Association for Talent Development (ATD) COMPLETE MAILING ADDRESS: 1640 King Street, Alexandria, VA 22314
11. KNOWN BONDHOLDERS, MORTGAGEES, AND OTHER SECURITY HOLDERS OWNING OR HOLDING ONE PERCENT OR MORE OF TOTAL AMOUNT OF BONDS, MORTGAGES, OR OTHER SECURITIES: None
12. FOR COMPLETION BY NONPROFIT ORGANIZATIONS AUTHORIZED TO MAIL AT SPECIAL RATES. The purpose, function, and nonprofit status of this organization and the exempt status for federal income tax purposes has not changed during the preceding 12 months.
13. PUBLICATION NAME: TD at Work (formerly Infoline)
14. ISSUE DATE FOR CIRCULATION DATA BELOW: September 2014

15. EXTENT AND NATURE OF CIRCULATION			Average No. Copies Each Issue During Preceding 12 Months	No. copies of Single Issue Published Nearest to Filing Date
a. Total Number of Copies (Net press run)			1253	1250
b. Paid Circulation (By Mail and Outside the Mail)	(1)	Paid/Requested Outside-County Mail Subscriptions Stated on Form 3541. (Include advertiser's proof and exchange copies)	486	606
	(2)	Paid In-County Subscriptions (Include advertiser's proof and exchange copies)	0	0
	(3)	Sales Through Dealers and Carriers, Street Vendors, Counter Sales, and Other Non-USPS Paid Distribution	714	599
	(4)	Other Classes Mailed Through the USPS	0	0
c. Total Paid and/or Requested Circulation (Sum of 15b. (1), (2), (3), and (4))			1200	1205
d. Free or Nominal Rate Distribution (By Mail and Outside the Mail)	(1)	Outside-County as Stated on Form 3541	0	0
	(2)	In-County as Stated on Form 3541	0	0
	(3)	Other Classes Mailed Through the USPS (e.g. First Class Mail)	5	5
	(4)	Distribution Outside the Mail (Carriers or other means)	0	0
e. Total Free or Nominal Rate Distribution (Sum of 15d (1), (2), (3) and (4))			5	5
f. Total Distribution (Sum of 15c. and 15e)			1205	1210
g. Copies not Distributed			48	40
h. Total (Sum of 15f. and 15g)			1253	1250
j. Percent Paid (15c divided by 15f times 100)			99%	99%

16. THIS STATEMENT OF OWNERSHIP WILL BE PRINTED IN THE NOVEMBER 2014 ISSUE OF THIS PUBLICATION

17. I CERTIFY THAT ALL INFORMATION FURNISHED ABOVE IS TRUE AND COMPLETE: Patty Gaul, Editor

JOB AID

PRIMARY LEARNER PERSONA (PLP) QUESTIONS

While not intended to be exhaustive, here a few categories of questions that may be useful as you and your project team create your primary learner persona.

Demographics of the PLP

- What is the PLP's name, age, race, and gender?
- What is the PLP's primary language?
- What is the PLP's educational background?
- What is the PLP's marital status?

Professional

- How long has the PLP been with the company?
- How often will the PLP apply what he has learned in the course?
- Has the PLP taken e-learning courses before?
- What type of computer does the PLP typically use?

Relevant Job-Related Information

- What other skills and abilities does the PLP have?
- How open to change is the PLP?
- Who does the PLP interact with daily?
- How far does the PLP commute to work?

Course-Related Questions

- How much training and experience does the PLP have with this topic?
- How does the PLP use social media?
- What other types of professional development does the PLP do?
- What is the PLP's preferred learning medium?

Personal Information

- Who would play the PLP in a movie about her life?
- What bad habit is the PLP trying to give up?
- What is the PLP's biggest pet peeve?